A Pet for Me

POEMS

Also by Lee Bennett Hopkins

I CAN READ BOOKS®

Sports! Sports! Sports! A Poetry Collection
Blast Off! Poems About Space
More Surprises
Questions
Surprises
Weather

PICTURE BOOKS

Best Friends
By Myself
Good Books, Good Times!
Good Rhymes, Good Times
Hoofbeats, Claws, and Rippled Fins: Creature Poems
Morning, Noon and Nighttime, Too
The Sky Is Full of Song

BOOKS FOR MIDDLE GRADE

Click, Rumble, Roar
Mama and Her Boys

PROFESSIONAL READING

Let Them Be Themselves
Pass the Poetry, Please!
Pauses: Autobiographical Reflections of
101 Creators of Children's Books

A Pet for Me

POEMS

selected by Lee Bennett Hopkins

pictures by Jane Manning

HarperCollins*Publishers*

ACKNOWLEDGMENTS

For works used in this collection, thanks are due to:

Curtis Brown, Ltd., for "Mornings with Midnight Blue" and "Pet Snake" by Rebecca Kai Dotlich; copyright © 2003 by Rebecca Kai Dotlich. "Homing Pigeon" and "Pet Love" by Lee Bennett Hopkins; copyright © 2003 by Lee Bennett Hopkins. Reprinted by permission of Curtis Brown, Ltd.

Madeleine Comora for "Ant Farm." Used by permission of the author, who controls all rights.

Fran Haraway for "Tarantula." Used by permission of the author, who controls all rights.

Avis Harley for "Hamster Hide-and-Seek" and "Puppy Olympics." Used by permission of the author, who controls all rights.

Lee Bennett Hopkins for "Cat" and "Goldfish Dreams" by Tom Robert Shields. Used by permission of Lee Bennett Hopkins for the author.

Tony Johnston for "Iguana." Used by permission of the author, who controls all rights.

X. J. Kennedy for "Dog Love." Used by permission of the author, who controls all rights.

Karla Kuskin for "I Would Like to Have a Pet" and "My Bird" from *Something Sleeping in the Hall* (HarperCollins). Copyright © 1985 by Karla Kuskin. Used by permission of the author, who controls all rights.

J. Patrick Lewis for "Just Fur Fun." Used by permission of the author, who controls all rights.

Marian Reiner for "Kitten Capers" by Aileen Fisher from *My Cat Has Eyes of Sapphire Blue*. Copyright © 1973, 2001 by Aileen Fisher. Used by permission of Marian Reiner for the author.

Heidi Roemer for "Hedgehog." Used by permission of the author, who controls all rights.

Alice Schertle for "Old Slow Friend" and "Turtle Thoughts." Used by permission of the author, who controls all rights.

Katie McAllaster Weaver for "Lullabies." Used by permission of the author, who controls all rights.

A Pet for Me: Poems
Text copyright © 2003 by Lee Bennett Hopkins
Illustrations copyright © 2003 by Jane Manning
Printed in the U.S.A. All rights reserved.
www.harperchildrens.com

Library of Congress Cataloging-in-Publication Data is available.
ISBN 0-06-029111-7 — ISBN 0-06-029112-5 (lib. bdg.)

1 2 3 4 5 6 7 8 9 10
❖
First Edition

To my great-niece
Kàyleigh Michele Yavorski
—L.B.H.

To Nellie, Crunch,
Whitey, and Toby
—J.M.

I Would Like to Have a Pet

BY KARLA KUSKIN

I would like to have a pet,

any kind at all.

Something big,

something small,

something sleeping in the hall

would be just fine.

I would like to have a pet.

Will you be mine?

Dog Love

BY X. J. KENNEDY

In the morning of each school day,

  on the corner,

Molly Mutt waits with me

  till the school bus stops.

In the afternoon when

  it carries me home again

she sits waiting till I come

    and up she hops.

She covers me

> with sloppy doggy kisses,

she licks my nose

> and lunchbox up and down.

Maybe other dogs, I bet,

> wouldn't get a kid so wet,

but I wouldn't trade

> for all the dogs in town!

Kitten Capers

BY AILEEN FISHER

He plays with anything he finds

and then if that should fail

my kitten never really minds . . .

he always has

his tail.

Old Slow Friend

BY ALICE SCHERTLE

All winter he sleeps

buried in the backyard

like an old stone.

In April,

he climbs out into the sun,

sprouts legs

like four stiff boards,

and crawls

across the garden,

my old slow friend,

remembering the taste

of lettuce leaves.

Just Fur Fun

BY J. PATRICK LEWIS

I set him on my elbow,

I put him on my knee,

I pet him with my finger—

My gerbil tickles me!

I know when he is hungry,

I feed him bits of seed,

And after dinner, there's a book

He likes to hear me read.

Pet Snake

BY REBECCA KAI DOTLICH

No trace of fuzz.

No bit of fur.

No growling bark,

or gentle purr.

No cozy cuddle.

No sloppy kiss.

All he really does

is hisssssssssss.

Goldfish Dreams

BY TOM ROBERT SHIELDS

Blast me gold.

Flip me fin.

Blow me bubble.

Wave me in.

Swish me tail.

Wink me scale.

Swing past castle
Trailed by snail.

Quiet swimmer

Deep dive home

Wrap in seaweed

Drift—

     Dream—

        Roam.

21

Mornings with Midnight Blue

BY REBECCA KAI DOTLICH

Most mornings we gallop

to Cragamore Creek—

she knows I have sugar;

she nuzzles my cheek.

I pick a sweet apple;

she whinnies and neighs,

then tugs at my arm;

she wants me to play.

We finally trot home,

pals through and through;

just me and my filly—

my sweet Midnight Blue.

23

Tarantula

BY FRAN HARAWAY

I would like a pet who's scary,

Who is very, very hairy,

But who's gentle

And as friendly as can be,

And who's happy when he munches—

Quite content with cricket lunches—

A tarantula is just the pet for me!

Homing Pigeon

BY LEE BENNETT HOPKINS

I wait

and wait

on this

hot summer day

for your return.

You know the way.

I clean your loft

your rooftop nest

where you'll

fly home

for

needed

rest.

27

Iguana

BY TONY JOHNSTON

I have a small iguana

the color of a lime.

He eats bugs for supper.

(He eats bugs any time.)

He blinks at me, so friendly.

He sleeps upon my knee.

I love my small iguana.

I think that he loves me.

Hedgehog

BY HEIDI ROEMER

Racing 'round his squeaky wheel
my hedgehog wakes me up.
I offer him a mealworm snack
and fill his water cup.

Wispy bits of cedar chips
cling to him—to me.
I stroke his spiked pincushion back
so so gingerly.

He's never learned to fetch or heel

or answer when I call.

Instead, he climbs my welcome hand

to snuggle in a ball.

Ant Farm

BY MADELEINE COMORA

Through glass I view a thousand legs

busy guarding precious eggs.

They shuttle loads of food to store,

then travel endlessly for more,

moving every grain of sand,

building bridges over land,

widening roads, closing them off—

the workers will not stop.

No one's time is ever free,

for all ants on the farm agree:

never rest or stop to play,

live to tunnel one more day.

My Bird

BY KARLA KUSKIN

My bird is small.

My bird is shy.

It does not sing.

It does not fly.

It does no tricks

and that is fine.

I love my bird.

My bird is mine.

34

Hamster Hide-and-Seek

BY AVIS HARLEY

Over my arm

she softly flows—

cinnamon coat

and whiskery nose.

With marble eyes

She stops and peeks;

lets me stroke

her knapsack cheeks.

Then ripple-of-fur

takes her leave

to probe new roads

inside my sleeve.

Turtle Thoughts

BY ALICE SCHERTLE

My turtle knows a secret,

I can see it in his eyes.

He's thinking

ancient turtle thoughts

mysterious and wise.

I keep his dish of water filled
for swimming and for drinking,
but his flat rock in the middle
is for sitting still
and thinking.

Puppy Olympics

BY AVIS HARLEY

Round and round
and round he goes
chasing his tail
in front of his nose.

40

Whirling in circles
a flurry of fur
spinning about
in a glorious blur.

Only a solo
but, oh, what a race—
to catch a tail
and win first place!

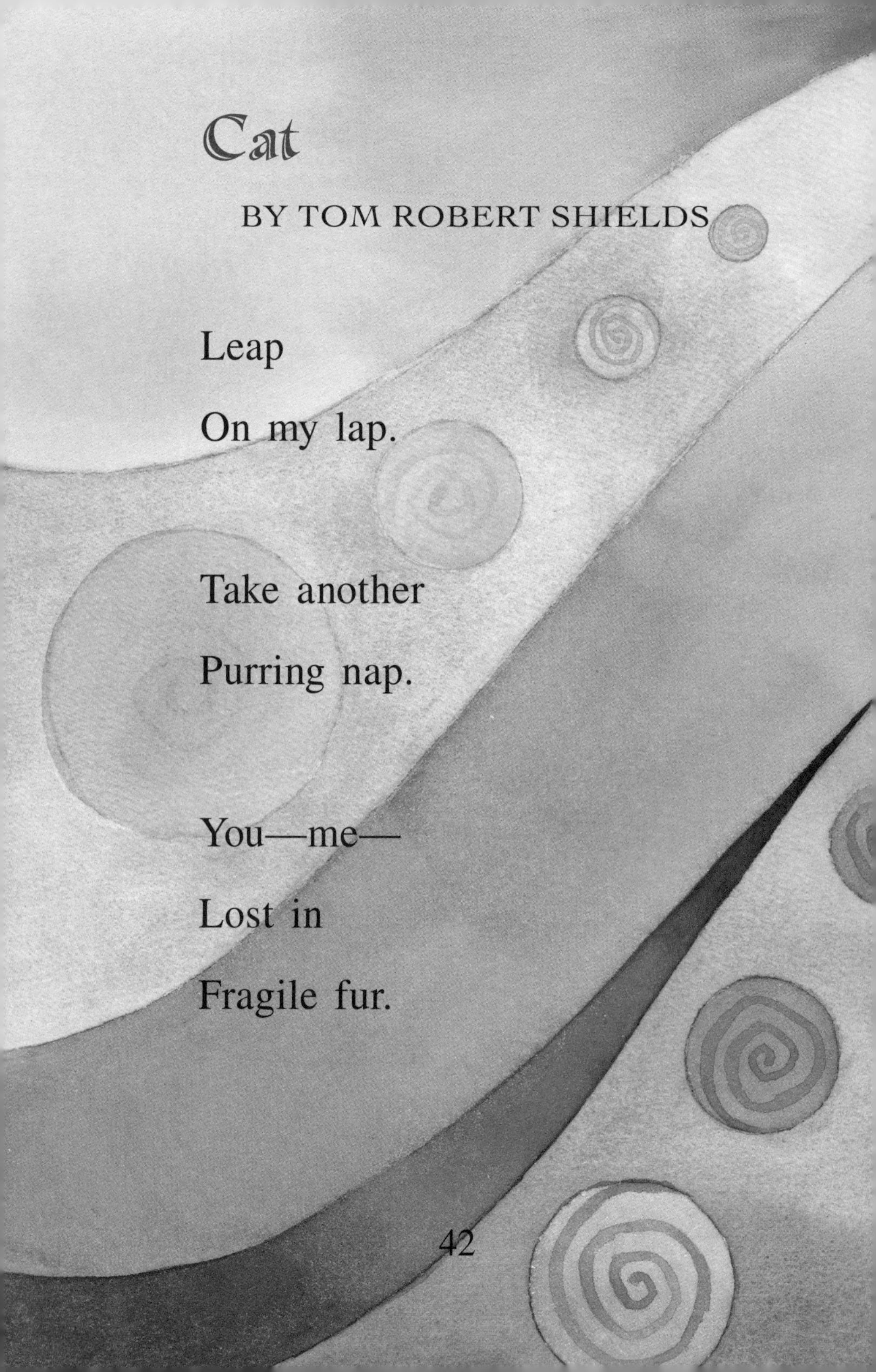

Cat

BY TOM ROBERT SHIELDS

Leap

On my lap.

Take another

Purring nap.

You—me—

Lost in

Fragile fur.

Why

would

we

ever

stir?

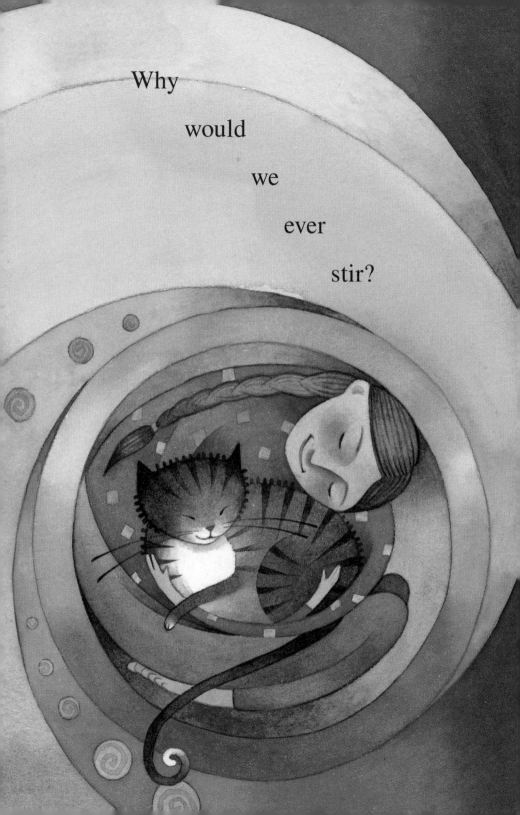

Lullabies

BY KATIE McALLASTER WEAVER

Late at night

my guinea pig

sings me lullabies.

She squeaks and chews

a song for me

until I close my eyes.

Pet Love

BY LEE BENNETT HOPKINS

All pets give love back

to you

in many

mysterious

wondrous ways—

wet kisses

soft hisses

snuggles

neighs—

through moments

through hours

of

pet-loving days.

Index of Authors and Titles